Gloriously Human

As Simple as A - Z

A. DEE HUXLEY

Published in 2020 by FeedARead Publishing

First Edition

Cover design by A. Dee Huxley
Logo design by A. Dee Huxley

British Library C.I.P.

A CIP catalogue record for this title is
available from the British Library.

for

All the weary dishevelled, and awakening, canaries across our beautiful planet Earth, Gaia.

It is time to spread those vibrant wings and fly. To seek new learnings and new adventures.

It's time to be Gloriously Human. This age ; this time and space in which we all live, demands it of each and every one of us.

It is nothing less than Gaia, our beautiful home, deserves.

For Her, for all my fellow human and non-human travellers, I offer you these guides ...

They have been the catalysts of my flight to a truer, healthier, and more authentic life ; receive from them what works for you.

But fly on the thermals of your own heart's desires !

With love,

Dee

Contents

Making Space

≈

Switch off all those devices that
connect you to the world *outside* of you.

It can be scary : but the world will be there,
when you switch all those sensors back on.

≈

Focus on your breath ; don't change it.
Simply become aware of the movement of air
coming into your body and the life-force
that breath contains. Be aware of your
exhale, as the warmed air leaves.

Notice the continuous cycle of the
movement of air ; your breath -
in - then out.

≈

Now you have created some time
for you. A *reconnecting pause* in your day.

≈

Smile, relax, keep breathing,
and enjoy ...

≈

Preface

Gloriously Human has evolved and coalesced into a synopsis of what I have discovered during my conscious attempt to follow a spiritual path, whilst living within a western secular society. Encapsulated is the realisation that we are essentially simple beings, (simple in the best sense). That we are at our wisest and happiest, when we listen to the small inner voice which always calls us back to our true essence.

As I travel my life's journey I become increasingly more aware of the common threads that bind us all. No matter how amazingly individual and unique our own personal course through life is - we share common threads - encounters with love, laughter, joy, peace, fear, sorrow, pain and death. As well as our shared longing for meaning and a sense of place, we implicitly seek the feeling of 'being home'.

I see *Gloriously Human* as a workbook, providing catalysts to initiate an honest dialogue with your own small inner voice. A pointer towards your own individual thoughts and feelings, helping to clarify questions or themes within your own daily life. Something you can dip into, as and when you feel.

If you are new to this form of meditation, or contemplative practice, journaling is a great place to start. Where you just simply consider a particular text that resonates with you, and let your pen be your guide. Allowing your rational mind to step aside so that you can connect to your emotional presence, your small inner voice, here in this moment of time.

Alternatively, you could initiate your practice by harnessing the power of intelligence-guided randomness. Discovered using the letters and numbers contained within this book, plus the 26-letters from a lexicon pack and a dice.

So this is a *not* a book that provides answers. Any external answers would be another's interpretation, and would probably not be the best fit for your own life. After all, at a deep level you intuitively understand that you already have all your own answers ; your own personal truths of how you want to live your life, and what really matters most to you. It is now time to chip away all of those aspects of your life that no longer resonate with your true nature.

Take pleasure in your own personal exploration, in your own discoveries.

And always remember, when we reconnect and become whole to ourselves, we are in part, integral participants in reconnecting to, and healing, *our fractured* world.

The Planting of a Seed

How many of us start our day truly believing, "Wow - another fantastic day in paradise !" I know I don't ; and I am probably not alone.

It came to me this morning, gently almost effortlessly ; my life is burdened, overloaded and complex. That is why there is no joy when I wake up.

How can I beam a welcoming "Wow !!" to my day, when the daily pattern of my life is : -

- Making an overwhelming array of minor and major decisions
- Being employed to achieve ever-changing objectives and targets
- Juggling money I haven't really got
- Balancing time and energy to be with my partner, with my family, with my friends, with the commitments of my career
- Trying above all, to maintain the persona of a human being perfectly at ease with themselves and with the world.

All this, whilst living entangled within a dysfunctional collective paradigm, which has only resulted in widening social inequalities and a detachment from nature's natural cycles.

The saying I'm 'not waving but drowning' springs eternal in my non-tranquil mind.

As I lie here in bed, (I haven't yet found the courage or the "Wow" to get up), I truly acknowledge that I have fallen down the rabbit hole of believing that my life cannot be joyful. Now I am a grownup, life *just is* complicated and difficult. I play the game of life - I pretend to be having a great time - I pretend to be coping - I pretend that they haven't hurt me. I smile - I laugh.

Now I fully realise that I am attempting to demonstrate to everyone, but especially most of all to myself, that I am happy. I mean really happy. I am doing better than most, so it must be working, mustn't it ?

But in my horizontal position a small, quiet voice joins in the conversation, "But what about the Wow ?" I instantly think, "Why don't you just leave me alone ?"

The gentle voice replies, "Because you feel exhausted. Because you are ill. Because you are sad. Because you are hurting". I lay in bed not wanting to move ; I wanted to hear more, much more. "Go on" I say, "you've got my attention".

The gentle voice continues, as requested, "You think life is complex and difficult. And as you look around you this view is confirmed.

Everyone is rushing around, achieving great and important things, forever busy. The world is an unremitting scene of activity, noise, disharmony and confusion.

But life wasn't designed to be that way. You were not designed to live that way. Life is really very simple.

You breathe in and out - you move your limbs - you eat to maintain your energy levels. You cry when you are hurting, (or at least you should). And you have an overwhelming desire to love, and to be loved. You have just forgotten, just mislaid, this fundamental truth.

And that's why I am here to remind you. *Life is simple. As simple as A - Z* !"

A

Action

Admitting

An

Analogies

Animals

A

A lot of what we worry about never happens.

And worrying is such a high-octane mind-blowing cognitive function that really impedes our thinking.

So be informed, strategise, plan - yes. But stop worrying.

Save that worrying-energy for dealing with what actually happens.

Action

Action

says the film director, kindly letting all the actors know when the scene is running.

But real life doesn't work like that.

Our thoughts patterns and actions lie at the core of creativity. So being the conscious artist in our own daily life is being an active participant in the ultimate creative industry : Life.

Admitting

Admitting

when we are wrong doesn't stop the world from turning.

It simply allows us to breathe more easily.

An

An

invitation should always be given, and received, with the right to say "no".

Analogies

Analogies

are immensely useful in allowing us to perceive things differently.

For example, if we were driving to work we wouldn't dream of following one car for five minutes, then choosing another car to follow for the next five minutes and so on. And then expect to arrive at our workplace on time.

We simply wouldn't do that.

So why on earth do we follow other people's opinions and expectations of our life and then expect that we will be truly happy.

Animals

Animals

are great healers !

Feel the fur then you will feel like doing anything !

Believing

Best

Big

Boundaries

Bringing

Business

Believing

Believing

is seeing. Some people think it is the other way around - that is, 'seeing is believing'.

But we can only see what we are open to the possibility of. That is why beauty is *truly* in the eye of the beholder.

Look well : don't become a mere scanner.

Best

Best

friends can also be found by simply looking in the mirror.

Big

Big

data flaps it's wings and no-one, absolutely no-one, should tremble.

Or change their decisions to be in vogue because an algorithm says so.

Boundaries

Boundaries

and empty space are exceptionally useful in our lives.

Not convinced ?

Then consider how useful a cup would be without a boundary and empty space.

Bringing

Bringing

a genuine "please" and "thank you" into our daily interactions, with an accompanying smile, makes us all feel valued. Those simple words and actions remain powerfully cohesive symbols.

People are people, living breathing individuals, they are *not* merely our service providers, or our staff.

Being polite is good manners, and good manners costs no-one and rewards all participants.

Business

Business

strategies have for far too long been based on the rules of competitive sports or war.

How about bringing engagement into the fold and dump the stuff that really doesn't work.

Changes

Choirs

Choreograph

Compassion

Conversation

Customers

Changes

Changes

in our mindset, in our paradigms, are extremely important for our personal and societal evolution.

Everything else is simply geography.

Choirs

Choirs

work best when everyone is singing from the same song sheet, and in the same key.

It is the same with any team working.

If we don't collectively know, or understand, the why (our purpose or aim), how on earth can we clarify the : who, what, how, where and when.

Choreograph

Choreograph

your own dance – who better than you to judge the steps and tempo of your dance through life.

So engineer your own choices ; don't become a driver-less car in your own life.

Compassion

Compassion

for all sentient beings *does* include being compassionate to yourself.

Being kind to yourself is the realisation that we *all* respond and evolve in the groundswell of understanding.

Berating others, and ourselves, closes our hearts to the living-compassion of our world. It leads to stagnation, inertia, disengagement and ultimately to the violent act of disconnection.

Conversations

Conversations

require active speakers *and* active listeners. Otherwise they are just simply monologues.

And of course, the best conversations are totally engaging. With all participants bouncing ideas, concepts and solutions, like radar, dancing on the waves of possibility in true dialogue.

And then the whole becomes greater than the sum of its parts. As personal intentions fuse towards the collective good, through the magical alchemy of synergy.

Customers

Customers

and employees, are the two sides of the same coin.

We can't have workable and sustainable capitalist systems based on companies wanting customers, whilst they are all simultaneously down-sizing.

Daily

Death

Delay

Democracy

Denying

Diaries

Daily

Daily

give thanks and praise for the life you *are* living.

So begin each day with gratitude for here begins a new life.

Death

Death

is the ultimate change manager.

So if we want things to be different when we, and that special someone, still reside on planet Earth : it's time to start that real dialogue today.

Delay

Delay

those hostile words for a few seconds – you might never use them.

Life is too precious, and sacred, for us to dig ourselves a metaphorical hole today, that we may never get out off. And think of all that sunshine we will be missing !!

Democracy

D4

Democracy

is a living, breathing, social contract.

The fundamental trust that makes democracy possible, is that those who govern will always have a 'Plan B', for the country as a whole, not just for themselves.

As a Gaelic name implies, it is indeed a 'crooked river' which navigates to undermine that bedrock pledge. One is especially found lacking, humming to oneself whilst walking away from a mess, a gargantuan, no-star Eton Mess.

Shame on you Sir ; because you fooled us once.

Denying

Denying

or shutting out the woes and issues of our world, turns us all into passive enablers for those who seek to lead through conflict and division.

The bullied should never have to stand up to the bully.

That is our role, the unbullied, the rest of us. Our silence, if given, is deafening ; taken by the perpetrators as compliance, acquiescence, perceived almost as a sign of cooperation.

We don't have to focus on the macro, within our own circle of influence we can be a beacon of hope and of change.

Resistance is definitely never futile.

Diaries

Diaries

are great to fill with events and people, but always remember that if you don't control your own diary someone else will.

And consider dropping some appointments. Your diary will forgive you !

Achieve more by doing less.

Eating

Erase

Estimate

Eternity

Everything

Extinction

Eating

Eating

nourishing food is fabulous, especially when shared with those we love.

But let's not forget that our minds, our hearts and our spirits require nurturing too.

Erase

Erase

bad memories.

Don't let your past rob you of your future ; or rob you of *this* present moment.

Estimate

Estimate

the likelihood of our species being deemed superior if the benchmarks were *not* determined by us.

Be humble.

We humans are just a strand of the web of life.

Eternity

Eternity

is a very, very long time. Stating the obvious ?

Sometimes the obvious needs stating.

Everything

Everything

that you see in the material world first came into existence as a thought.

And we can all agree that any object ; a chair, a table, a car, a house - all had an designer, a human being that was the original creator of the concept.

The natural world is infinitely more complex that any object a human mind has ever designed. Ergo, it is not exactly a quantum leap to consider that the natural world also has a designer ; an ultimate creator.

Extinction

Extinction

of humankind remains a possibility.

Don't live as if it's a foregone conclusion, or a non-starter.

Be responsible : be mindful.

Failure

Feast

Fence

Follow

Forgiveness

Friends

Failure

Failure

only comes in one form.

That is failing to carry on, giving up before we have achieved what we set out to do.

Everything else is simply feedback ; a potential for learning.

However, making sure that we do *listen* is key to the usefulness of that feedback. We don't want to waste time doing exactly what we did before, whilst expecting a different outcome.

Feast

Feast

on the wonders of life ; you'll never go hungry.

Fence

Fence

no-one into your life using the words of love.

How many times do we say "I love you", which then comes consciously or sub-consciously with a list of expectations and anticipations. Be aware, be mindful ...

But also be aware and mindful of those fence posts, and fence panels, going up around you.

If they are already there ; then go ahead and create your very own metaphorical gate. Go through it and look back on that scene.

Only you can decide whether it's a safe haven or a prison - and when you know *that*, you will know what to do.

Follow

Follow

your own dreams ; be a seeker and a finder.

Fly on the thermals of your dreams. Live as the eagle, who seeks the deepest blue of the sky and stretches upward to touch the face of God.

Forgiveness

Forgiveness

of ourselves and others is essential for a happy and abundant life.

That forgiveness doesn't actually *condone*, or *deny*, those past words or actions.

It simply stops us putting any more toxins into our own mind and body.

And remember, we are not giving ourselves, or others, a licence for mind-less repetition.

Friends

Friends

and family are the stars of our lives.

Let's invite them all around for a party, switch off the lights and admire our very own night sky !

Gaia

Gloriously

Gossip

Governments

Gratitude

Graveyards

Gaia

Gaia

is a living sentient being, and is our gracious and immensely generous travelling companion.

That's a given.

However, what kind of symbiotic relationship do we want with Her ?

Must be mutualism of course. After all we don't want to be thought of as parasites, do we.

Gloriously

Gloriously Human

are two words on a page - a concept of the mind.

Become a living, breathing movement in and across time and space. We are all so much more than a mere name, or label.

Gossip

Gossip

is harmful ; don't engage in it.

It diminishes both the speaker and the listeners. And it really is a waste of everyone's time and breath.

If we have an issue with someone, then having a meaningful conversation with them is infinitely more productive and can elicit real change.

Governments

Governments

become more than sound-bites.

Now that you have become the ultimate risk-takers ; the lenders of last resort to the volatile financial markets ...

embrace being the facilitators of sustainable change.

Believe in, and engage with, your citizens and create the societies and communities that we all want to live within.

Gratitude

Gratitude

is a living, every day philosophy and way of life. It is not easy though.

And so here are a few tips.

> I think, therefore, I am grateful.
> I see, therefore, I am grateful.
> I love, therefore, I am grateful.
> I am loved, therefore, I am grateful.
> I laugh, therefore, I am grateful.

And I have saved the biggie for last -

> I can breathe, and yes I am here ; therefore, I am *truly*, grateful.

Graveyards

Graveyards

are full of people who were not told that they were loved
when they were alive.

So cherish those whom you love.

And tell them in every which way, with words and deeds,
how much you love them – they may not always be with you.

Help

Hereditary

Holograms

Houses

Humans

Hymns

Help

Help

someone across the road by all means ; but only if they want to cross, and only if they have asked you.

Don't disempower others by taking over unnecessarily.

You will instinctively know when someone *really* needs your help.

Hereditary

Hereditary

is not an excuse - it's a starter for ten.

Holograms

Holograms

express the whole within a part.

Our individual thoughts and actions can either passively reflect, or actively influence, our societies.

The one *is* the many.

Houses

Houses

become homes when love is not a guest but a resident.

Be at home everywhere you go.

Humans

Humans

were given a mouth and language in order to convey to others our inner landscape. To speak from our heart so that others may know us and that we may find our tribe.

When we do not stand up for our beliefs, especially in situations where individuals are denying another's rights, then part of us dies inside and our light is dimmed.

Better to speak and be judged harshly by others than to judge ourselves lacking in both beliefs and courage.

Hymns

Hymns

of praise are heard in forests as well as in cathedrals.

The choir just looks a little different.

If

Incessant

Integrity

Intel

Intermissions

Is

If

If

we truly want to change the world we, as individuals and as societies, have to stop rewarding reckless and bad behaviours.

And always remember that our ultimate trump card is not to play along.

Incessant

Incessant

noise and chattering drown out the important.

So isolate yourself from others for a few minutes every day – it's not detachment, it's meditation.

13

Integrity

Integrity

is the light in the darkness - the beacon in the night.

Your very own north-star shining brightly here on Earth.

Intel

14

Intel

get great market share for having the fastest processor.

But that doesn't mean that there are any significant benefits for you being the fastest in town. Skidding around and copious multi-tasking are not very sustainable, or in fact, very efficient.

Busy is not always best.

Intermissions

Intermissions

in life's play can be the greatest source of learning.

Don't be afraid to put yourself on 'pause' sometimes.

Is

Is

there any thing more important than :

Being

Here

Now

Doing

This

If we don't recognise the importance of the 'here and now', we may in the future come to see how glorious that place and moment, and those people and animals, actually were.

Use now-sight instead of hind-sight to capture life in 'real-time', and enjoy those precious moments while we are living them.

Jewels

Jobs

Jostle

Journeys

Junk

Justice

Jewels

Jewels

are discovered when you fully embrace the essence of your true nature.

First : reduce, then eradicate, the self-sabotage, (you know exactly how that manifests for you).

Then the healing, the alchemy, begins ...

Jobs

Jobs

are not excuses to give up our dreams. Don't have a slog-a-job life !

Jostle

Jostle

no-one to get where you want to go, you won't enjoy your destination.

Journeys

Journeys

improve with the right travelling companions.

Junk

Junk

mail is annoying ; junk thoughts are harmful.

What are you thinking ? What are you feeling ? What are you are believing ? Know yourself.

Justice

Justice

requires total impartiality ; justice for all irrespective of an individual's rank, connections or finances.

When we *truly* enact that in our legislation, and *truly* apply it in our law courts, in our workplaces, in our homes and in our hearts ; then the meek will indeed inherit our beautiful Earth.

Kind

Kindergartens

Kindred

Kneel

Knock

Knowing

Kind

Kind

thoughts heal the world – beginning with you.

Kindergartens

Kindergartens

sometimes look like tower blocks. Don't get involved with office politics.

Kindred

Kindred

spirits are life's greatest joy and life's greatest sorrow :
it's the price of *truly* sharing yourself.

Kneel

Kneel

or bow your head daily in humble prayer.

It does not have to be in front of an altar : try a tree, an animal, a river, a mountain - anything that inspires you.

Knock

Knock

and the door will be opened, but remember to go through !

Knowing

Knowing

how to evaluate assets, liabilities and opportunity costs is the bedrock for any personal choice and is key to having any form of abundance in our lives.

And that knowledge goes way, way beyond the financials.

Language

Laughing

Life

Love

Loyalty

Luxuriate

Language

Language

is exceptionally important !

It determines how we perceive ourselves and how we perceive our world.

Language can be concepts-based or actions-based.

Look at the world through the eyes of verbs not nouns ; through being, through doing, through seeing, through listening rather than through merely naming.

And always remember : language is only meaningful when we speak, and listen, from the wisdom of our *own* heart.

Laughing

Laughing

at ourselves occasionally is extremely healing.

In a pivotal time and space in Earth's history it helps not to take ourselves too seriously.

It is also the best tonic to ensure that we don't become too self-centred or too narcissistic.

Life

Life

is simple and joyous !!!

It is, however, easier to remember that in some situations than in others.

So be extremely mindful of -

Who you are with
Where you are
What you are doing

And most importantly : Why you are there.

Love

Love

really does conquer all ; even death.

Loyalty

Loyalty

begins with being loyal to your own values and principles.

After all they are the only things that keep you truly unique.

Remain a brand ; don't ever become a mere commodity.

Luxuriate

Luxuriate

once in a while in the miracle of simply breathing.

Mammoth

Melodramas

Mindsets

Misguided

Mistakes

Moment

Mammoth

Mammoth

tasks overwhelm even the most courageous – the trick is to break it down to manageable pieces.

One step at a time !

Melodramas

Melodramas

have a life of their own. That is, they don't need our presence.

Mindsets

Mindsets

are exceptionally important in determining how we perceive our world. But our concepts rarely represent the full gamut of reality.

For example, if we *see* grass as 'greener on the other side of the street' then we are perceiving an optical illusion, due to the refraction of light.

If we *think* that grass is 'greener on the other side of the street' then we are experiencing a cognitive illusion, due to not knowing all the facts.

Grass is green here, and there. In fact, grass is green everywhere.

Walk your talk : be open : be humble : be mindful.

Misguided

Misguided

individuals in the spiritual community carelessly refer to the realm of reality, which we call space and time, as an illusion.

No-one, absolutely no-one, has the right to refer to another sentient beings' pain and suffering as an illusion. That is, to deny that it is happening.

However, they are quite at liberty to rise above their own pain and suffering, thereby being a living example of their own faith.

Mistakes

Mistakes

and flaws provide great compost for growth – accept that and relax.

But keep growing - keep learning - keep evolving.

Moment

Moment

by moment – that's how life is truly lived.

Be physically *and* psychologically present in the moment.

So if we can't be psychologically present, best for all involved that we are physically absent too.

Negative

Never

No

Nostalgia

Not

Nurture

Negative

Negative

thoughts never create positive results.

Never

Never

mistake kindness for weakness.

No

No

is a very under and misused word.

Being clear about who we are, and what *truly* nourishes us, makes the use of the word 'no' infinitely easier and significantly more life-affirming.

Nostalgia

Nostalgia

is great sometimes, but always remember the people and events that are with you *today*.

After all, we can't drive our car solely by looking in the rear-view mirror.

Not

Not

for the lack of trying should your dreams slip away.

Nurture

Nurture

the spiritual within you and all will be revealed.

Offered

Often

Omens

Once

Only

Owning

Offered

01

Offered

a freebie ; examine the price tag very carefully.

And preferably *before* you accept.

Often

02

Often

we condemn others for *our* own greatest mistakes.

Omens

03

Omens

or, crucial gestures and words, are usually only recognised in hindsight. Be mindful.

Once

04

Once

we look for God we'll find Him, (or Her), in the most unexpected of places.

Only

05

Only

the foolish have no fear – action despite fear shows true courage.

Owning

06

Owning

our finances is infinitely better than our finances owning us.

Wealth, is synonymous with money. And yes totally, there is absolutely nothing uplifting, individually or societally, about the lack of money : homelessness, food banks, living on the bread line, or not being able to pay our way. Yes true wealth does include our finances for sure.

But true wealth is also about so much more ; it's about life, connections, love, friendships, meaning, community and values. And anything else that personally makes our hearts kinder and our lives enriched.

Pagans

People

Perseverance

Personal

Play

Pondering

Pagans

Pagans

were *never* heathens – their temples were simply not built by man.

People

People

usually want what they don't have.

However, we can only be nourished by what we *actually* have.

Perseverance

Perseverance

is holding on ; when holding on is all that's left.

Personal

Personal

and societal evolution, usually comes either through pain or awareness.

When we have lived enough pain, we begin to become sensitive to the possibility of learning through awareness.

Play

Play

and authentic laughter feeds us whatever chronological age we are.

Pondering

Pondering

on our own mortality occasionally – helps us to clarify what is *really* important.

Quacks

Quality

Quantum

Quick

Quietly

Quote

Quacks

Quacks

like a duck ?

Then you know the rest. Don't allow yourself to be fooled by the obvious.

Quality

Quality

relationships make us stronger than we can be on our own.

Foster them, nurture them and *always* delight in them.

Quantum

Quantum

physics, the electro-magnetic spectrum, shows us that everything is ultimately pure energy, vibrating at different frequencies.

That is, the rate of vibration determines what is visible, or invisible, to human perceptions.

This is not abstract conceptual theory - it's physics. And yet we continue to live exclusively in the material world.

Or do we ?? Humanity harnesses these invisible laws every day ; connecting two inanimate devices through Wi-Fi signals.

There is always a transmitter and a receiver. You just have to be on the same wavelength !!

Quick

Quick

harsh words – leisurely regret.

Quietly

Quietly

decide what *you* want before others choose for you.

Quote

Quote

from any spiritual text by all means. However, living it every day is much better.

Be authentic : be accountable : walk your talk.

Rarely

Reason

Reducing

Remember

Robots

Rustic

Rarely

Rarely

is the path towards enlightenment smooth and trouble-free.

But looking back along that path gives you the knowledge that it could have been *way easier*, both for yourself and for others, particularly for those who *really* love you.

Don't give up, or mourn past regrets, keep going with joy filled steps and a grateful heart, the best is yet to come ...

Reason

Reason

alone is never enough – seek the missing component.

Have a real conversation with your heart. Be more than artificial intelligence.

Reducing

Reducing

the suffering of all sentient beings begins with taking ownership of our own life.

Remember

Remember

only what is joyful, or what is useful.

Robots

Robots

already exist in many large organisations.

They are disempowered people just 'going through the motions'. However, human beings are not designed to live like that. We are designed to be fully engaged ; to seek to add value for the greater good.

If our organisational cultures are designed by, and reward, the self-seeking, the ego-centric of society, then the rewards go the few and the costs are incurred by the many.

A really great paradigm, or 'field of play' for social cohesion, excellence and evolution !!

Personally I think not : what are your thoughts ??

Rustic

Rustic

is art without artifice.

Real art doesn't have to reside in galleries, in museums, in private collections, or even in warehouse storage facilities.

The mighty hand of tides juxtapositioning a piece of driftwood possesses the quality of uplifting beauty. If we take the time to really look.

And in nature, the emperor is *always* fully clothed.

Scale

Silence

Slow

Sorrow

Space

Spreadsheets

Scale

Scale

is an imperative factor in how our perceptions are shaped.

A single strand of your hair doesn't recognise the gloriousness that is you.

So don't beat yourself up too much, but it really is time to recognise that you are a single baby curl on the body of Gaia.

And yes, like you, She *really* is a living sentient being !

Silence

Silence

is a great antidote to anger, particularly of our own anger at a perceived oversight or slight.

Don't feed the fire with even more fire. Focus on the breath and retain equilibrium.

Firemen rarely use fire to put out a fire.

Slow

Slow

down and take time to soak up the view. We will never again experience these people and events exactly like this.

We have earned the right to pause, seek the subtle nuances and have our Spirits refreshed and renewed.

And remember to smile and relax. We have earned that right too.

Sorrow

Sorrow

is an ingredient of life – however, only accept the measure required for the recipe.

Space

Space

and time for ourselves. Now that's a purchase worth making.

How can we invest and spend wisely - in terms of our time, our energy, our knowledge and our money - if we don't really have time to understand our *true* desires.

Spreadsheets

Spreadsheets

are the number-crunching marvels of the world. They seldom, however, tell us the whole story.

The bottom-line is usually, as the name implies, at the bottom.

Look up, see the actual living-breathing people, see their talents, see their possibilities, and human-crunch for a wee while.

And lo and behold the bottom-line looks way more profitable.

Taste

The

There

Thinking

Timing

To

Taste

Taste

your food – remind yourself where it came from and give praise for it sustains you.

The origin of our food-chain is *always* our beloved Mother Earth ; Gaia.

Thanks Mum !

The

The

people who truly hear you, only need you to whisper.

If you are shouting then find other listeners.

There

There

is no such thing as an inconvenient truth. We all know that to be true.

The truth is *always* the truth.

The inconvenience simply comes from the timing of that truth. Particularly when that unwanted truth is inconveniently delivered today.

Thinking

Thinking

of others before yourself is fabulous ; but don't become either a victim, or a martyr.

Timing

Timing

is everything. Spring *really is* Spring.

Listen to the seasons of our Earth and of your heart.

To

To

the journey !

Enjoy the process, don't exclusively focus on the hoped for, or anticipated, outcome.

Unconditional

Understanding

Unimportant

Uniqueness

Uphold

Use

Unconditional

Unconditional

love – we all yearn for it but few of us even consider giving it.

Understanding

Understanding

the difference between natural laws, and the human-made constructs of our societies, is fundamental to an expanded consciousness of our world.

Clearly there is no 'economics rock' out there.

There *are* other ways that we can choose to live.

Unimportant

Unimportant

thoughts and actions can become very important with hindsight. Be mindful.

Uniqueness

Uniqueness

is not an excuse for disharmony.

Uphold

Uphold

your Higher Self – your ego is dispensable, your Soul is not.

Use

Use

your wisdom well – don’t condemn it merely to a monetary transaction.

Vandalising

Verbs

Verdicts

Victories

Visible

Voicing

Vandalising

Vandalising

our home, Mother Earth – arrogance and stupidity gone mad.

Verbs

Verbs

in the English Language are 'doing' words.

So don't live your 'life' simply as a series of nouns, just naming and labelling ; places, people, animals, trees and every other mini and macro eco-system you come across. Embrace the aliveness of 'life'.

Live your 'life' as the greatest verb of all -

> Walk your talk
> Speak from your heart
> Do what you say you will
> Don't rely upon the empty promises of others
> Be authentic
> Be accountable

Verdicts

Verdicts

of guilt or innocence are not always made in a court of law.

Be careful not to judge.

Victories

Victories

achieved at the cost of losing our own true values are not victories even worth considering.

Visible

Visible

is only the tip of the iceberg.

But what's not explicitly revealed, (our individual and collective covert beliefs and emotions), have an incredibly potent impact on our lives and on our environments.

After all, Titanic was fatally wounded from below the surface.

Voicing

Voicing

our true beliefs is based on the sound proposition that the universe, and we ourselves, are always listening.

We

When

Where

Which

Why

Wisdom

We

We

are *all* body, mind and spirit.

The most significant impact in our life is which of those triple aspects is our principal driver.

When

We

are *all* body, mind and spirit.

The most significant impact in our life is which of those triple aspects is our principal driver.

When

When

the world is viewed from the mind there are many truths.

The heart knows there is only *one* and speaks with one voice, if allowed to do so.

Where

Where

the 'rubber meets the road' can be a very deflating place.

Especially if we are under another's, (or in fact our very own), metaphorical tyre.

Always remember that thoughts, emotions, words and actions have consequences. Be wise.

Which

Which

do you want, a great eulogy or a great life ?

Of course, it is never an 'either, or' choice. A great life creates a great eulogy ; at the very least for ourselves.

Why

Why

do people think that God, Source, Great Spirit, or however we perceive our Creator, would want us to live with poverty, suffering and war. Living our daily lives, and working within, unequal hierarchies governed by the few primarily for their own benefits.

Why would someone think that ?

No ; we are all born equal in the eyes of our Creator. And all of us are given the gift of free will.

The rest comes post-birth.

The conditioning, the dividing up, the greed, the selfishness, the desire to win-at-all-costs ; these are all human-made creations. Therefore, we can choose different ways of living, both individually and collectively.

Wisdom

Wisdom

comes to those who have the courage to wait, and listen, to the silence of their *own* heart.

Xamine

Xcellence

Xhilarating

Xploit

Xternal

Xtreme

Xamine

Xamine

all your promises very carefully ; preferably *before* you make them.

Xcellence

Xcellence

is witnessed daily by you. Don't believe me ? Then look at a flower in bloom.

Xhilarating

Xhilarating

in the joys of others increases our own happiness.

When we smile, we are making connections and have discovered the secret of perpetual motion.

Keep smiling ; faces, eyes and hearts.

Xploit

Xploit

no-one ; and that includes yourself.

Don't dismiss anyone's feelings, or to deny anyone their dignity or their hope.

Xternal

Xternal

actions and our feelings are ultimately determined by our internal thoughts. Think well !

Xtreme

Xtreme

measures are rarely required. Softly, softly, works wonders.

Yachting

Yearning

Yokes

You

Youngsters

Your

Yachting

Yachting

is an excellent metaphor for life.

The tiller needs little correction to have a dramatic impact on your course.

Yearning

Yearning

for yesterday, or tomorrow, does not change anything.

Living today and doing things differently changes both our future and our past.

Yokes

Yokes

remain only because we accept them.

You

You

can make life infinitely easier for yourself !

We all know that it is far less stressful boarding a ship when it's docked in a harbour.

Think ahead - consider consequences. Foresight is not that extraordinary if we have been 'down this road' before, and we usually have in some way or another.

Youngsters

Youngsters

are intuitively drawn to what, and who, feeds and nurtures them.

As we grow older we suppress our intuitions. Reclaim the wisdom of youth.

Your

Your

garden can teach you everything you need to learn about the ways of the universe.

Step outside your door, relax, commune with Mother Earth and enjoy the lessons.

Zebras

Zenith

Zero

Zest

Zoom

Zoos

Zebras

Zebras

are lovely creatures beautifully adorned with black and white stripes.

They are also perfect reminders that computers exist within a binary world of '1s' and '0s'.

As with the zebra, real-world situations are far more nuanced than simple black and white, 'yes' or 'no' answers. And yet 'the computer says no' mantra increasingly invades our daily living.

Also we never get to know who coded *that* algorithm, or even how many people *actually* understand its logic.

Zenith

Zenith

aspirations enable us to aim for our highest goals and ideals.

Any journey does indeed begin with the first step ... and is in essence a sequence of steps across time and space.

But each of those individual steps *always* occurs : here and now.

So remembering to enjoy each step of our journey, being fully present to the here and now, is the pinnacle of consciousness.

Zero

Zero-Sum

scenarios, are really only based upon the mindset that for a winner or winners there must be a loser or losers. The 'winner takes it all' is such a narrow and tedious viewpoint.

But fortunately they are not the only games in town. Widen your perspective to positive sum scenarios ; create win-win situations.

However, key to any success is knowing the rules and choosing the players to game with.

Life : game on !

Zest

Zest

for life keeps us young, whatever our chronological age is.

Zoom

Zoom

in on -

Beautiful sunrises and sunsets
Eyes shouting "I love you"
Flowers oozing complex simplicity
Glorious giggling joy
Hands waving hello and goodbye
Meows and woofs and other interesting chats

Allow yourself to notice the extremely important as well as the urgent.

Zoos

Zoos

are the modern day's Noah's Ark !

Now totally necessary in order to retain the genetic bank of our fellow travellers. But remember that they were brought into existence by humankind's arrogant stupidity.

And Finally ?

Human beings are only a single strand of the web of life ; and so, irrespective of our social and financial status, we are *all* welfare dependents.

That is, we are utterly beholden to the generosity of our diverse eco-family : the fauna, the flora, the water we drink, and the very air that we breathe. And of course, the land we live our lives upon, which also feeds our bodies and nurtures our spirits.

We are embedded within our Earth's natural cycles. That fact is so blindingly obvious, so up close and personal, that somehow we consciously forget that during the milieu of our daily activities.

But our ancestors knew with every fibre of their being - that they were inextricably connected to the soil, to the animals, to the birds, to the plants, to the trees, to the rivers, to the seas and to the air. They knew that their well-being, their very survival, depended upon healthy and sustainable eco-systems.

When we humans migrated to the cities of stone, glass and steel, we believed it was our natural birthright, our entitlement, to raise ourselves up, to evolve. And that is what we were meant to do, to evolve ; but not to conquer.

We have not risen above nature ; we cannot - because we are part of nature.

Instead we ventured alone ; soaring to the pinnacle of human folly. Those self-proclaimed dizzying heights starved us of the essence that makes us human. We lost ourselves in a human-constructed myopic maze, of synthetic classifications, isms, schisms, ideologies and labels.

Our citified-psyche insidiously severed us from the living primal force that binds us all. So we have evolved deformed.

Lauding our rational mind, whilst diminishing our intuitive heart, and even denying our spiritual essence - any sense of the sacred. And when nothing is sacred, we unwittingly create a wasteland for us all : then we are *all* in survival mode.

a different way.

consciously choose

But we *can*

Importantly in life, we can relook, glimpse what we thought we knew, and see through fresh eyes.

And life itself is lived at its best, on the 'pathless way' ; on the wave of possibility, ∞. There can be no beginnings, without endings, for each ending spawns new life ; new beginnings. That is the way of nature. It is the way too, of our individual and collective lives, if we open ourselves to the gloriousness of our nature within.

Our personal and collective healing begins when we turn aside from viewing our Earth, and all our fellow travellers, through the grasping lenses of instrumental value. And move towards embracing our gloriousness through gratitude and humility ; viewing our Earth, and all our fellow travellers, through the loving eyes of intrinsic beauty.

So let us give thanks and gratitude for the love and insights we gain along the road that each of us must travel. But we never have to journey alone ; for we all have the capacity to reach out, share our common humanity and what we have learnt along the way.

And we all do learn ; either through pain or awareness, from the greatest teacher of all, the academy of Life.

But ultimately in time we all do graduate - through, and for, love.

Our painful scars transformed when we love and forgive ourselves, and each other. For love and forgive we must ; because there is still a lot of living to do !

So let our Spirits soar with the eagle, our hearts and feet connect to the living presence of our precious Mother Earth, *our hom*e ; cocooned within a canopy of Grace.

Just Actions

≈

We all come from the one Source

≈

Love yourself : you are magnificent

≈

Love all life : we are all magnificent too

≈

The Earth is our most precious gift - do not abuse Her -
or we will be evicted

≈

Humans are but one strand of the web of life : respect
all our fellow travellers

≈

Believing is seeing : believe in Peace. Be Peace-full

≈

≈

Do not go with-out : *Be Still and Look Within*. Behold how beauty-full you are : how beauty-full everything is

≈

On a daily basis say "thank you" to all the Earth's trees and plants, for they really do gift to you the very air that you are breathing *now*

≈

All appliances - yes even our smartphones and our tablets - come with an 'off' switch.
Use your devices well : don't let your devices use you

≈

We are *all* body, mind and spirit. Each needs to be allocated space and time to be nurtured and nourished

≈

≈

Multi-cultural societies include nourished fauna, flora, water, air and soil, as well as nourished humans. Be mindful : be kind

≈

Be authentic. Walk your talk : speak from your heart. Then others will know you, and you will know yourself

≈

Gratitude is a great way to start your day. For here *really* does begin a new life

≈

Remember, reclaim, your "Wow".

You are part of the web of life, you matter.
And, even when you don't think about it, you live
each day with your wonderfully diverse planetary family,
on a spaceship that is your glorious home ...
Mother Earth, Gaia.
And *they are* the web of life.
So they all matter too.

So live and breathe a life that is in harmony with
nature's compassion, generosity and love.

Become Gloriously Human ...

About the Author

Dee believes that we are increasingly living our lives entangled within 24/7 market-based societies.

Our home and work environments have become bastions of information and distraction overload. Where our five senses are incessantly bombarded by a stress-producing human-made ecosystem ; one that drowns out an inner spiritual life, or denies its very existence.

She also passionately believes that the ethos and values of the Celtic, Native American and Taoist traditions remain pertinently valid and increasingly more relevant in today's globalised but disparate societies. These traditions teach us how to create a space for inward connection, a 'time-out' from externally-focussed living, so we can harness our own intrinsic values and provide clarity of purpose to our daily actions.

As part of her own 'slow down' life change, Dee left a long and successful career in UK central government when she recognised that she could no longer be an agent of positive sustainable change.

Dee now lives in coastal Wales, with her partner and furry friends. She now focuses on listening to nature's rhythms and continues her study of these ancient traditions.

Dee shows us the true nature of relationships, and the continuing impact of the misaligned, but dominant 21st century human-centred narrative, whose elemental dynamics is fracturing all of our relationships.

Our relationship with ...

ourselves
other human beings
our multi-species planetary family
our planetary home
Great Spirit

Dee's books -

Footprints In Time	(2017)
Whispers Of Life	(2018)
Gloriously Human	(2020)

Printed in the USA
CPSIA information can be obtained
at www.ICGtesting.com
LVHW051548141223
766375LV00003B/262

9 781839 454776